Fragile Global Hope…

ISBN 978-976-8203-80-9

Introduction

We all have hopes and dreams as long as we are alive. If we are ill, we hope for the day when we will be well again. If we are going through some difficulty, we dream of the day when this too will have passed.

There is a universal hope that the world will one day experience once and for all, lasting peace. However this hope is like a mirror which is very fragile and is liable to break anytime by the actions of the same people with this hope.

Fragile Global Hope…

Acknowledgement

I would like to say thanks to my friend Peter Neil and my cousin Dahlia Robinson for their contribution to this work. Special thanks goes out to Maurice Goldson my brother in Christ for his continued encouragement and support.

CONTENTS

The Physical Man

As a Man Thinketh

Have you ever thought

What life would be?

All your thoughts and plans

Rolling on a square tube screen.

Or, when you think

As the computer system shouts,

Your secret endeavours show up

As hard copy print out.

Lives are unfolded

From mustard seed thought,

These we see blossom

Fruits mankind has brought.

So be clever in what you do

Cultivate healthy thoughts,

Show the world who you are

Never accept nought.

You see whatever a man conceives

It's hard for him to hide,

As he cunningly slips from his mind

He is caught in stride.

<u>As He Enables</u>

I raised my head from the pillow,

Smiled again another day,

His loving hands guiding

Facial muscles

That says, thank you Lord.

Up and about

Without mechanical aid,

Eager to face today's darts

Knowing full well he who woke me,

Will again enable.

With firm and steady stride

I move through the door,

Armed with the assurance

As I breathe,

He is ever near.

I greet you with a smile

And my mother was ill,

Radiotherapy, Chemotherapy

One set of foot prints,

The river flows continually

For God enables.

With integrity I praise

Being respectful and kind,

Allow his light to shine

From a gentle embrace,

Or shout by doing a fair days work.

COUNTER ATTACK

Overload with endless possibilities

Reading tell-tale signs,

Of greed and deceit

Thoughts launched in your direction,

Explosions in your head,

The enemy has launched another round.

Read the instruction manual

Put on the breast plate of righteousness,

Pick up the shield of faith

Don't forget the helmet of salvation,

Launch your counter attack

With the potent word of God.

DI PRICE FI LIFE

Rain a fall

Dutty tuff

Jesus dead pan di cross

Between two cruff

Di soldier dem a laugh

Him clothe it rip off

Woman hole dem belly and bawl

Waaaaaaaaay!

Him neva trouble nuhbady

Dem charge him fi blasphemy,

But is not that,

Is talk fi mi Him talk fi mi

Dem kill Him because Him talk fi mi;

Him sey Him come fi give mi life,

Politician, Religious fanatics give Him a fight

Him sey Him come fi liberate

Dem kill Him, sey is evil dem hate

Which evil, man still a create.

Rain a fall

Dutty tuff

Jesus dead pan di cross

Between two cruff

Di soldier dem a laugh

Him clothe it rip off

Woman hole dem belly and bawl

Waaaaaaaaay!

But is earth runnings

Him did tell dem still

Sey the temple woulda dismankle

Den reassemble in three days

Cow inna pasture a graze;

Him look down from di cross

And although Him a feel pain

Him still coulda have sympathy

Cause Him did know bout prophecy.

Rain a fall

Dutty tuff

Jesus dead pan di cross

Between two cruff

Di soldier dem a laugh

Him clothe it rip off

Woman hole dem belly and bawl

Waaaaaaaaay!

But dem stanup and a mock Him

Jeer and spit pan Him

And Him mother, she couldn't tek it

Bredda John him couldn't stop it

But Him Faada di building Him shake it!

Run and fret weak heart

Now that the place get dark

Mek wi si who have the last laugh.

Rain a fall

Dutty tuff

Jesus dead pan di cross

Between two cruff

Di soldier dem a laugh

Him clothe it rip off

Woman hole dem belly and bawl

Waaaaaaaaay!

Now the doubters all have faith

Everyone believe Jesus is great

Yet some a wonder

Still a ponder

Why Him neva come down from the cross

Box down two soldier who did a laugh

Lead a coup fi overthrow Ceaser

Understand yu fi understand yu leader

Life is not thirty piece a silver.

Dem sell Marcus Garvey

Fi rice and peas

Today dem a sell Jesus fi bun and cheese

Fi him life worth more dan fi a King

The Lamb of God

Tek weh all a wi sin

The Lamb of God

Tek weh all a wi sin.

<u>EXCUSE</u>

I came to praise you Lord

But the benches are hard,

I came to praise you Lord

And the sermon was cold,

I came to praise you Lord

My friends wore new clothe.

I came to worship you Lord

My heart was strangely warmed

As the choir sang

I came to praise you Lord

I confess

I don't know how.

<u>Finding Rapture on a Lonely Shore</u>

It's the singing of the heart

At the taste of sweet simplicity,

In the face of the awesome vastness

Of the sea.

It's watching an empty milk-box

Being washed in v-lines along the shore,

It's gazing carelessly

At the breaking waves.

It's listening to the endless roar

Of the waters,

While digging into wet sand

With your toes.

Rapture in the feel of the strong

Sea wind

Blowing your hair loose.

It's smiling with the open sky

While the sun burns your back,

It's finding society where none

Intrudes.

It's not being so hateful as to

Think of something as serious

As life,

Thus smashing the delicate glass of

This rapture on the shore.

Dahlia Robinson

<u>Friends</u>

Friends are

Like flowers in the garden

Of love,

Nourished with the radiance

Of understanding,

Protected and sought after,

With the innocence of youth.

From Here On

I will see my renaissance,

Die to earth

Live in spirit land,

No more ifs and maybe

I will do

What must be done.

Ride the waves,

Climb the mountains,

Or walk around,

I will arise

And go.

From here on

I will be a new being,

A flower in the garden

Of life,

I will be a success

From here on

I will shine

For those in the cave,

The smoke behind the

Mountain.

From here on

I will love because

Of love

Yet not my will,

His blood and my

Faith are joined.

Dedicated to Wenise Davis

Have you seen Him

Have you seen Him as He passed this way?

Which way went He, tell me I pray

Did you feel His warmth, did you see His smile

Have you touched His hand reaching to thine?

Did you hear His voice even as you prayed?

Did you see Him? Did you see Him? I need Him today.

Have you seen Him, that moment of truth?

Have you knelt before Him, broken or astute?

Did you see your life in the mirror of His eyes?

You cry for mercy and know it's alright

All that came to Him, none did He cast away

Did you see Him, Did you see Him? I need Him today.

There are some things, which to me, take forever

But to wait on Him, My pleasure!

I have no hope if He is gone never again to see

How sure am I, knowing He walks with me

Where have you gone my hope and my strength?

Did you see Him? Did you see Him? I need Him today.

Peter Neil

<u>HERE ARE THE KEYS</u>

Here are the keys Lord

You take over,

Here are the keys Lord

You drive

I know not where I am going.

Here are the keys Lord

Open the door,

My heart's hinge seems to

Have stuck,

Pour your oil of grace on them

Now enter in.

Take charge oh Lord

Of my life,

Be the road map I so desperately need,

The guiding lights

On the runway,

Direct my safe landing I pray.

IN LIFE - DEATH

Oh death,

You are a part of life

Life, a part of death

A day has night included,

Bitter sweet the reality.

The earth sits on an axis

After sadness

Comes the morning sun

Breathe life into the growing seed

That was dead.

In death there is life

A dead seed

Sprouts with newborn energy,

Be not afraid

See the rainbow through the rain.

In death there is life

Oh my brother, my sister

Weep no more

Look beyond, the pearly gates

Are open

A bright light shines forth,

To die in Christ is much gain.

<u>Ivan the Hurricane</u>

Like a ship

Whose rudder snapped lose

Hurricane Ivan drifted towards Jamaica

The crew on land bowed and prayed.

With intermittent reports

How closer and closer it came

Security measures went into action

Hammers and nails worked together,

Money and food exchanged position

And men scurried to and fro.

SOS, SOS

Went out from land and sea

As the Ivan ship slowed

The chief captain stood at the wheels

Not wanting to crash land

Took over control

Broad siding it along the south coast.

The howling wind

The pelting rain

Encircled the house,

Like a prowler trying to get in,

Woo, woo

As it searched for a weak opening.

LIFE'S LIKE THAT

There's a mountain on the highway

Rivers rushing beside,

Some sit at the base

Others a hasty retreat makes,

Some stand to contemplate

Others kneel and pray.

A tiny ant

Years ago did arrive

Slowly makes its way

Over stones, blades of grass

Rest today.

Carried by the wind

Always looking ahead,

Said he

"Sugar covers the valley."

<u>Listen</u>

Have you ever wondered

Why things said passes you by?

Things you wish you'd remember

An aid to love and life;

Stop the constant blabber

Listen a little bit more

When you talk too much

You'll never hear yourself snore;

Continuous rambling over works

The jaw bone

Clogs the ears

Disconnects the phone.

Life could be so much better

If we listen a little bit more.

LIVING EYES

O Son of man I cannot believe

You have eyes but cannot see,

You look at me and still you can't see

How I am a part of God's family.

I looked at you and turn mine eyes

Raised my head and heart to the sky

As my body and tattered garments revealed

The unseen poverty raging in me.

I thought that your help was near

By how you looked and the way you steared,

But surely the twin mirror of your mind

Pictured the selfish thoughts I could not find.

O son of man how can you love God

When you turn your back on the needs of man,

Life so busy you cannot be late

So the poor beggar man just has to wait.

But living eyes sees your

Needs all the while,

Pass your shallow garments

And superficial smile,

The mouth of your heart is your eye

And indeed living eyes,

They don't lie.

Lord you are Wonderful

The open sky,

With its cool, serene and lushus blue,

Where the birds forever fly

And many a man longed to do,

Lord you are wonderful.

The tall cedar trees to care

The mountains in all their splendour,

Lilies bulbous with fragrance

Beyond compare,

Lord you are wonderful.

Little streams, rivers, and the great

Oceans

The land and all its creatures,

And man,

Yes man in the image of God,

Spiritual features,

Lord you are wonderful.

That's what nature says

Lord you are indeed wonderful!!

<u>RESCUED IN TIME</u>

The water was up to my neck,

I closed my eyes,

I was sinking in deep mud

Never knew the danger

Of deceitful pleasure

Quicksand smelt like rain-damped earth.

The lies were

Chocolate covered stale nuts,

I closed my eyes tight

Going down felt like floating

My throat felt dry,

I swallowed but,

Began to cough.

My sins oh God

Are not hidden from you,

You see how foolish I have been,

To those who trust you

Don't let me bring shame,

To those who worship you

Don't let me bring disgrace.

The strong arms of the Lord

Reached out like the almond tree,

As the pain and heartache

Pierced into my flesh,

Pulled me up,

The waves rushed in to cover me.

The Choice is Yours

Choose you this day

Whom you will serve

You and only you

Must choose,

Win or lose, you must choose.

To take this bus

Wait for another,

You and only you

Must choose,

Early or late, you must choose.

Take a break now

Work straight to your end,

You and only you

Must choose,

Confrontation or healthy life you must choose.

To abstain now

Go all the way,

You and only you

Must choose

Sweet to the taste bud or lasting dreams

You alone must choose.

Your colour be neutral

Unless prostrate you lay,

You and only you

Must choose

Stop at the red light

Go through the amber

You alone must choose.

The earth is the Lord's

With all its bounty

You pick from the tree

Fact or fiction,

Eternal damnation, everlasting connection

You alone must choose.

To rescue the soul

He died on the cross

Faith asks, do you believe he is;

You choose to say

I will not choose,

by not choosing,

You made your choice.

The goodness of God

(Psalms 36)

Lord, your constant love reaches

The heavens

Your faithfulness extends to

The skies.

Your righteousness is towering

Like the mountains

Your justice is like the depths

Of the sea.

Men and animal are in your

Care.

How precious o God is your

Constant love

We find protection under the

Shadow of your wings

We feast on the abundant

Food you provide.

You let us drink from the

River of your goodness

You are the source of all life

And because of your light

We see the light.

The True You

You can wear the cloak

Of righteousness,

From sunrise to sunset

Decked from head to toe

In your public image gown,

But when the moonlight shines

In your bed you wrestle

With conscience,

You undress the memories

You are confronted with

Private image,

The true you.

Will you be ashamed

Of your nakedness?

Will you be ashamed of you?

WE MUST GET UP

We must get up
Can't sit down

If we want to reach down town,

The ground dove isn't like a light pole

God made man with a soul.

We must get up

If we want to reach,

The Julie mango

On top of the Fridge

To lick the juice running down your hand,

You must open your big mouth man.

We must get up

If we want a job,

Wishing and hoping, lying in bed

Put on your clothe, open the gate

Exercise an ounce of faith.

We must get up

Plant a tree,

A simple task you will see

Starts the train or bus a rolling

Stops the children's belly from growling.

Do something with your

Hand or mind,

Get up man, make a move on your feet

Don't sit there let your heart stop beat.

What Life Can Be

I visited a desolate Island

Its streets were almost bare,

Sake for the many signs and bill boards

Scattered across the landscape.

How is your attitude today?

Did you forget your prayer deposit?

Remember to show gratitude,

As I drove on the high way.

It got much more interesting

As I turned on a side road,

Did you check on your neighbour?

I will bless the Lord at all times

His praise will ever be on my lips.

Stop

Check your emotions,

Do your heart test today

Are you loving someone?

Take the load off

Give away something nice

For a change.

Strange enough I asked myself

Where could everyone be?

This seems a great place

For mankind to be.

Alas I was awakened

By the sound of children's laughter

Innocent souls beaming light and joy

And what life could be.

I asked a youngster by the road

Are there no commercial signs

In town,

His broad smile told

I was a stranger

Pointing to one

That said,

Always test your scale and balance.

WHAT'S IN A TOUCH

HEALING POWER!

Cried the bleeding woman

Pushing through the crowd,

Vision!

Echoed the Bethsaidan man

Standing o so proud,

A smiling touch can do a lot

This I've seen said Bartimaeus.

Music to my ears!

Sang the man from Decapolis,

A touch oozes cleansing power

The man with leprosy insists,

A gentle touch

Can change so much

Whispered the daughter of Jairus.

Amen!

Sang the widow of Nain

Indeed a touch says a lot

I must confess, the best

Antibiotic we've got,

Touching is so tender and real

It's the story of life we feel.

Yet a common message flows

From every friendly touch,

Convinced I am and very sure

Human love to be touched

It says so much.

WHO CAN MEASURE UP

God, who can stand before you

Who can say, "I have been good"?

In the face of your life

Our living is like grass.

For when we smile at all

We have done

Your goodness outshines all

And we are nothing.

So who can be like you?

Who can truly achieve your status?

He that has clean hands

And a pure heart

Yes Lord, wash us clean

Make us pure.

WHOSE FAULT

The earth is dry

The sun reigns,

The grass is brown and

The throat it pains

Ethiopia cries from Africa

And her tears are dry like the Sahara.

She sends her surplus

Across the Atlantic

Into the land of her children's

Children

And the cry is louder, so frantic

The winds have died

The oceans swell with measureless tides.

No light, no food, no doctor

No bus, no gas no water

And the fingers point in opposite

To find the true and sly culprit.

Yes the fingers are right

Pointing we are three times correct

Within the heart the problem starts

Each man his thoughts must not forget.

How we dramatize our thoughts

Living every day

Plays an important part;

Times we just wouldn't pray

Carelessly we went our way.

Yes it is our fault

You and I and everyone,

It's time we change our selfish ways

Lift up our hearts to the needs of man,

If we love God, let us now be willing

To serve our fellow men.

The Physical Man

A KISS

A kiss is a kiss

Whether French or vanilla

A hug is a hug

Whether bear or Asian

The universal language

Is spoken through a smile.

A laugh is a laugh

Whether husky or raunchy

A smile is a smile

In Alaska or Africa

Love is love

Now or here after.

Bully- Mi nu like Yu

Mi hate yu

Mi no love yu

Yu a bully

Jus a push an' a pulley

Mi no like yu

Mi a guh fight yu.

Woman malice man

Cause a yu

Married life mash-up

Sake a yu

Yu a bully

Jus a push an' a pulley

Mi no like yu

Mi a gu fight yu.

Look pan yu work

Inna Africa

Malnutrition

Inna Jamaica

By di sweat of mi brow

Mi a gu beat yu

Lick yu wid hard wok

An' little bandoolu.

Mi nu like yu

Mi a gu fight yu

Yu choke nuff a wi

Wid white squall

Nuff hungry pickney

Gu to bed a bawl

One day poverty

Mus' fall

When fi mi life style

Grow tall.

Mi hate yu

Mi no love yu

Yu a bully

Jus a push an' a pulley

Mi no like yu

Mi a gu fight yu.

Too long mi a feel

Yu pressure

All mi try

Tings a get tuffa

So much family

Yu mek a suffa

Price increase

Nu mek it any betta.

Yu shoot ghetto youth

Dem nu wear suit

Some depend pan loot

And yu find dat cute;

Cause yu a bully

Jus a push an' a pulley

Mi nu like yu

Mi a gu fight yu

Box kick an' bite yu

Wid nuff dollars

Mi a gu beat yu.

Culturally Mature

She danced mento

Sang Rock Steady

Reggae and Soul

Shook the body of many

Laughed with Mass Ran

Oliver Sam

This beauty queen of the Caribbean.

She wiped away Shakespeare sweat

With pantomime River Mumma

Golden Table cloth

Somewhere in Jamaica

Along Naesberry Street

No more setting

In London sleet.

Yesterday America's Grammy

Did not foretold of

Jamaica's Jami

Music videos

Soft and loud

Jamaica forty-five and still proud.

Ripe is the time

Miss Lou dons the crown

Bob Marley and Garvey

Celebration abound

Land of wood, sun and water

Awakes from its slumber

Now an international daughter.

Eruption

No superficial signs

The sun shines

No earth shaking evidence

While the pressure builds.

Traffic running to and fro

Watching the plane in the distance

Engaging the right persons

Smiling without a strain.

Overhead bridge holding strong

Standing upright unassisted

Daily heat rising from the pavement

Sweaty palm change in body temperature.

An instant rumble

San francisco's road explodes from within

Heart attack stroke you down

Hypertension and earth quake

Shatters the normal day.

<u>FRAGILE GLOBAL HOPE</u>

The fear of the dragon

Babylon the powerful

With your embargos and restrictions

You sentence the globe for being round.

Their armies are linked

Across the dessert with unseen chains

That binds them together

Forever in their squalor

Of pride and self.

To be most powerful

Your brother is powerless

There is no master

Without a servant

Who placed him on the throne?

Justice for all

Justice for none

And guns and bombs deepens

The divide

Cutting a wider chasm

In this fragile global hope.

Happiness is an Excursion

A cloud of doubt hovered around

Our plans and ideas uprooted from

The ground

Still we journeyed onward without complaint

O God

Please hold back the rain.

We stopped in May Pen for awhile

Exchanged a few words and a couple

Of smiles

Still the day was silent as we

Pushed aside

Our fears, loneliness and pride.

Then a sudden change at the bath

When food told hunger

Please depart

So up and onward to the beach

A great surprise awaited each.

Along the sand we dragged our feet

Dancing to the tune of four

Hearts beat

Laughing and jumping from rushing waves

But by the boats we had to bathe.

Then back to May Pen I heard my name

Who could it be now playing game

I looked up, smiled and kissed

Her face

Sadness today, happiness has replaced.

A long lost friend was all

I need,

To make my day complete indeed

Such beauty and sunshine

Smile

Grace I met from across the miles.

I Write Again

It feels good

Touching once more,

Feeling again

Heart racing with

Pleasure again.

I write again

The lyrics flows

Like the God bless Jordan

Pouring down like rain.

Kissing again

Fresh new lips

Inspires again;

Writing again with caution

Creating each word with care.

<u>Imagine</u>

Imagine a nation under siege

People running to and fro

A country arrested

Bombarded by crime and violence

Cornered by the flood of murders.

Imagine searching for clues

Fingers pointing outwards inwards

Politicians, Deacon, Businessman

Bin Laden, the Police Force.

Imagine living without values

Life without a road map

A matter of survival

Bread and butter maybe it

Society sets the menu

Serves the dish.

Imagine your schools philosophy

Life is measured by how you live

What you give

Not what you have

Yet who receives the respect

Mister wealth need not join the line.

Imagine the perfect sermon

Is the one you live

Acquire your Lexus, Rolex, and SUV

The respect will come along

By all means

Acquire the whole world

Try not to lose your soul.

Imagine a mixed up world

Serving a two course meal

Equality on the table

But justice is held in a side room

For the selected few,

Your invitation is bigger than mine.

Imagine open warfare to

Acquire the symbols of wealth

Imagine jailed by false doctrine

Without knowing

Having acquired all these

Your rapture comes too soon.

Kuh Pan Mi

Kuh pan mi

A walk pan di street

Kuh pan mi

Nuh have nutt'n fi eat

Kuh pan mi

A nuh me did dweet

Kuh pan mi

Cho yu see't.

Kuh pan mi

A walk up an' dung

Kuh pan mi

A come mi jus' come

Kuh pan mi

Use to work dung town

Kuh pan mi

Dem waan mi fi lie dung.

Kuh pan mi

Use to work inna bank

Kuh pan mi

Work as a civil servant

Kuh pan mi

Always mi give t'anks

Kuh pan mi

Bwoy, dem jus cut rank.

Mi se kuh pan mi

A my time now

Kuh pan mi

Hey bwoy, yow!

Kuh pan mi

A try fi hide di frown

Kuh pan mi

Cho, mi a go dung town.

Let the People Know

There was a programme on TV

It identified high and low

Accusations and denials

They called it Portfolio.

Then there were conversations

Between men of Church and state

They too had to answer questions

On the programme Face to Face.

It had a chief moderator

Who sometimes play a bit tough,

Knows how to pick the brain,

Goes by the name Wilmot.

He tried his best at times

To bring out into the light

The reasons, facts and failures

And why things aren't that bright.

Today the issues are alive

Across the globe in the park

With intensity and passion

A moderator just as Sharpe.

Natty – Dread

Natty!

Yu wanted

Natty!

Yu faith dead

It bitta Natty

Life dread.

Yu wanted fi murder

Yu kidnap and rob,

Di verdict pass before a trial

Natty

No freeness caan help.

But yu not di only murderer

Natty, yu have company

Dem drive easy Benz and SUV

Yu haffi tief it.

Yes, Natty

Gulf war come

Dem raise dem price

Natty dem tief jus like yu,

Madda caan feed har pickney

Not yu dis time, Natty

Not you.

Politicians

In conspiracy

Wid capitalist worshippers

Done kill off nuff poor people,

Natty, yu have company

Dem hunt yu dung.

Dem freeze wi wage

Let loose free enterprise

Dog fi nyam wi;

Suck out wi blood,

Some survive some way.

Natty!

Yu wanted

Natty!

Yu faith dead

It bitta Natty

Life dread.

SCHOOL BAG

I just don't remember

Cannot recall

School bag did I have

On my journey through

Rousseau Primary.

Now it may seem simple

Probably strange

But I just don't recall

Seeing me with

A knap sack.

We did common entrance

Studied from Junior English

Revised

But maybe just maybe

I cannot see in retrospect

One book in a bag.

Today school bags turn holsters

History, books and marbles

Concealed

Alas unannounced we arrive

At the shrine of shotters and dons.

Liberation god unlocked long ago

The gates of barrel children

TV god parents

The lessons were university taught

Respect the bling and blinger.

But they have no head for academics

Tuff head illiterate dunce

Cannot tek the book so

Why not learn a trade

Look at their army skill.

From Trench Town to Ricketts avenue

Illusive is the school bag

Water soaked books,

Matches sticks racing in the gutter river

And shoes wrap-up under clothe.

So watch the bags

How they hold the books

Not all the youths are studious

The shape of the mind is taken from home

The community must take hold.

The Convert

Di system

It hurt,

Di system

Mi waan eat dirt;

Di system

Blouse an' skirt

How times rough

Nat even likkle hussling

John face an' tripe a twis'.

Stop chat fallee tee

Bout system

Get up,

Fin' wok

Yuh lazy good fi nutting;

Watch me

A ghetto tree

Growing towards the sun

Moving from di gutta wata.

But wait

Ghetto tree...mek yu ben' so?

How yu leaf dem so brown?

Mi nuh waan sey it

But yu look run dung;

No rain naa fall

Wata lock off;

Di system

Weh yu sey?

Di system?

The People's Court

Justice will fall down

Like rain,

Truthfulness like the roaring sea

Yet the people cried,

Crucify Him, Crucify Him.

Convicted even before a trial

Condemned before a spoken word;

He threatened the very fabric

Of a political system

He shook the foundation

Of a Religious Order,

By His life.

Crucify Him, lynch Him

Hang Him on a tree

No thought of possible innocence;

Chase him, grab him

Beat him till him soft

Put a tyre around him neck

Light it.

Justice will fall down

Like rain,

Truthfulness like a roaring sea

In the people's court

Your innocence is your fate;

As cold as death.

THE WALL

Standing there looking, I pondered in my heart

Why are you here, was the question in my thoughts

Walls protect, walls hide, walls they separate

Walls keep out, walls lock in, walls block, walls stop

Walls slow down.

Walls talks, walls hurt, walls shoves around.

Walls stand, never moving, always resisting.

So wall are you proud? To be the one who discourages,

Who keeps mankind down?

Walls are tall, walls are short, they are black and white

Bearing stones, blocks and various designs.

Are you not the same? Where you not there yesterday?

All my years growing you have always been the same!

Oh wall, it must stop! Freedom will come Alas!

Peter Neil.

. **Tommy Dies**

When we were young, we had such fun

Watching the tides and the evening sun.

Minutes to hours, hours to days and days to months

As if time never mattered.

Marbles you did love and cricket a specialty

At school or the streets all challenges you did beat.

Among others you were the one, the 'don.'

There were no dons in our days, all were safe

'Till someone said, 'why not become one?'

Alas, our world took its shape.

We did what we did, said what we said

To all we were tough. Shed no tear, laughed no laughter

Specialising in making fear.

How we toiled hard to build a reputation.

Fighting almost back to back,

It was a sad day when you died; all hope now, was lost

I was there; saw in tears a face of unbelief

You held my hand trying desperately to speak.

What were you saying, to a lifelong friend - 'Goodbye,' 'I'll miss
you', Or 'WHY?'

And so I too must be gone,

I too am on a run, for now with

Tommy gone, I fear his friends will find me.

Peter Neil

Vantage Point

It never moved, it laid still

No sound preceded, no dreams fulfilled.

I wondered why, where could it be?

Being here, but yet not

Seen but unseen, heard but unheard.

Filled with tears, sorrow, unhappiness

Joy, bliss, hope and love.

It contradicts itself, for here is death but life

Hopeful but without hope

No return, but sure to return

Where is it, where does he really lie?

Is he really here or there, did he really die?

The dead are gone but they are not,

Where are you? Where are you?

Surely not in the grave.

<u>War for Peace</u>

In the middle

Of the east

They brought guns

To make peace;

From the west

Came the best

So they claim

By their test.

But the Arabs

Were no coward

History showed their

Suicide squad;

With nothing to lose

Fight to the end

They choose.

Now the Bush

Was serious;

The Sadam

More furious

And none would ease up

Until the silent

Night erupt.

Scud missiles

B6 bombers

Painted the night's sky

And patriots with

Rocket launchers

Scattered the ground over.

WHEN LIFE WARS

Poverty I loath

With its terrible blows

Of hunger and nakedness;

Without notice it slaps you in the face,

Kicks you in the stomach,

Dictating the path you must go

Then it seems

You are angry with the world,

Probably everyone around you

And each man is an enemy,

The cause of your loneliness.

Wi Know What a Gwaan

When wi si di jeep

a crawl down di street

wi know what a gwaan;

when di youth get two inna him skull

and no eye witness

wi know what a gwaan.

Watch di politician

A walk through di community

wi know what a gwaan;

Five years ago wi hear the same story

wi know what a gwaan.

Hey shotta wid di glock

Nobadda pitch pan dis tree

wi know what a gwaan;

Wi naa defend that

Unnuh si a school ting dat

wi know what a gwaan.

Missa tailor get contract fi build highway,

Him pants fava three quarter drape

wi know what a gwaan;

Three card man sometimes dress up inna suit

Unnuh fete him at Pegasus, and tink dat cute

wi know what a gwaan.

Forty five years wi living wid anancy

Inna di jungle yu learn fi survive

wi know what a gwaan;

Watch we a di stoplight a beg a ting or two,

We write di chapter and verse

So we know what a gwaan.

<u>Writing Made Easy</u>

I've never learnt to write a poem; neither do I possess the skill

But somewhere deep in the shadows of the human heart

A desire, a strong desire – to do what? Express myself

Let me see, I don't know the words to say, and what others do

I don't understand

I've tried everything else, so now I'm writing this poem.

And somehow it begins to happen, as a doors swings open

With words and tears joyful and sad.

Why a tree, why a cross, why to die

Listen, please listen was His reply….I love you.

Now, is praise made easy and finishing this poem a joy?

Peter   Neil

9 789768 203809